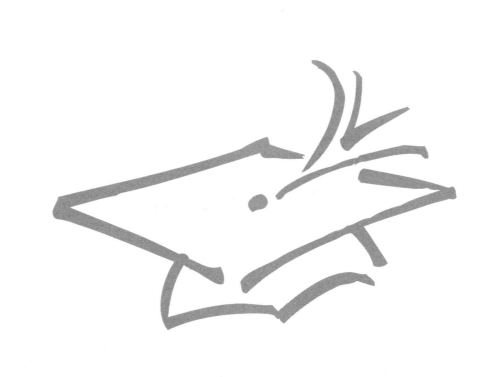

To

_____

From

_____

Date

_____

Our purpose at Howard Books is to:
Increase faith in the hearts of growing Christians
Inspire holiness in the lives of believers
Instill hope in the hearts of struggling people everywhere
Because He's coming again!

Published by Howard Books, a division of Simon & Schuster, Inc.
1230 Avenue of the Americas, New York, NY 10020
www.howardpublishing.com

101 Most Important Things You Need to Know Before You Graduate © 2008 by Renae Willis

First Howard trade paperback edition February 2008

Library of Congress Cataloging-in-Publication Data
Willis, Renae.
 101 most important things you need to know before you graduate : life lessons you're going to learn sooner or later— / Renae Willis ; illustrations by Dennis Hill.
    p. cm.
 1. Conduct of life—Miscellanea. I. Title. II. Title: One hundred one most important things you need to know before you graduate. III. Title: One hundred and one most important things you need to know before you graduate.
  PN6338.C65W55 2008
  081—dc22

2007018545

ISBN 13: 978-1-4165-4982-6
ISBN 10:   1-4165-4982-X

10 9 8 7 6 5 4 3 2 1

Manufactured in Mexico

For information regarding special discounts for bulk purchases, please contact: Simon & Schuster Special Sales at 1-800-456-6798 or business@simonandschuster.com.

Edited by Chrys Howard
Cover design by Dennis Hill
Interior design by Stephanie D. Walker
Illustrations by Dennis Hill

To Meredith and Anna,
who have taught me
about life's most important things.

1

"It's not about you."

—*Rick Warren*

2

It may not be the race
you thought you entered,
but it's the race you're in.

3

"Do not hide your light
under a bushel basket."

—Matthew 5:13–20

4

Conduct yourself
and dress yourself
to show respect for YOU.

5

"The world would be
a much cleaner place
if everyone swept
in front of
their own door."

—*Mother Teresa*

*In other words,
mind your own business.*

6

"Some days you're the bug,
some days you're the windshield."

—Author Unknown

*Life is not fair;
don't expect it to be.*

7

"Mistakes are part of being human.
Appreciate your mistakes
for what they are:
precious life lessons
that can only be learned
the hard way.
Unless it's a fatal mistake,
which, at least, others can learn from."

—*Al Franken*

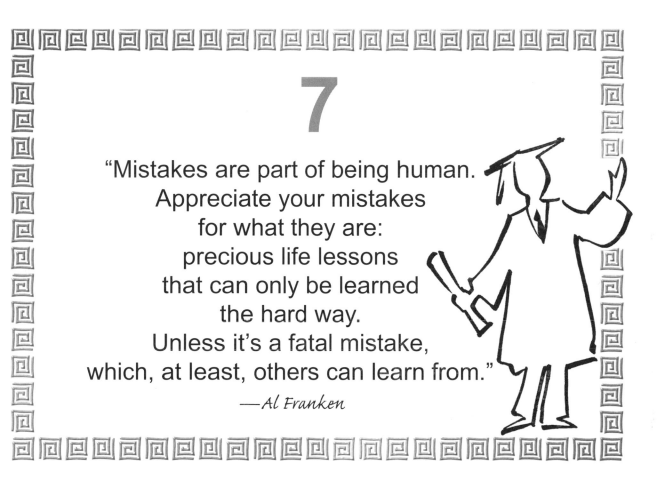

8

"Make new
friends,
but keep the old.
One is silver,
the other is gold."
—*Joseph Parry*

9

"Generally speaking,
you're not learning much
when your lips are moving."

—*Author Unknown*

10

"To whom much is given,
from him much will be required."

—*Luke 12:48* NKJV

11

"When I stand before God
at the end of my life,
I would hope that
I would not have a
single bit of talent left
and could say,
'I used everything you gave me.'"

—*Erma Bombeck*

Glorify God by using what you've been given.

12

People will forget what you said,
people will forget what you did,
but they will never forget
how you made them feel.

13

"Wisdom is the quality
that keeps you
from getting
into situations
where you need it."

—*Doug Larson*

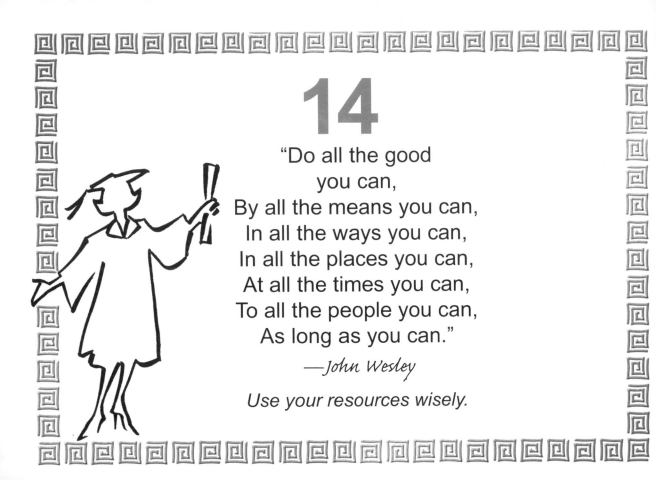

14

"Do all the good
you can,
By all the means you can,
In all the ways you can,
In all the places you can,
At all the times you can,
To all the people you can,
As long as you can."

—*John Wesley*

Use your resources wisely.

15

"Any day that you
have a doorknob
on your side of the door
is a good day."

—*Former Vietnam POW*

*There is always something
for which to be thankful.*

16

"Be like a postage stamp.
Stick to one thing
until you get there."

—*Josh Billings*

17

"Keep your words
soft and tender,
for tomorrow
you may have to eat them."
—*Author Unknown*

"*You cannot unsay a cruel word.*"
—*Author Unknown*

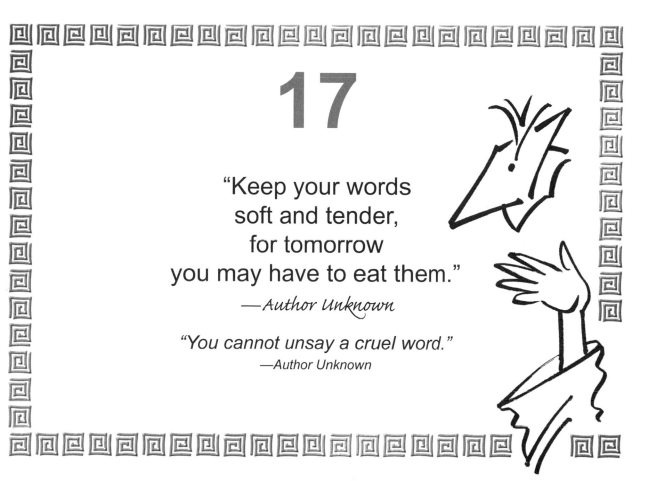

18

Have the willpower
to say "no"
when you need to,
and the courage
not to feel guilty about it.

19

Leave things
better than you
found them.

20

Life is
so much simpler
when you tell the truth.

21

"The ugliest personality trait:
selfishness.
The most worthless emotion:
self-pity.
The most destructive habit:
worry."

—*Author Unknown*

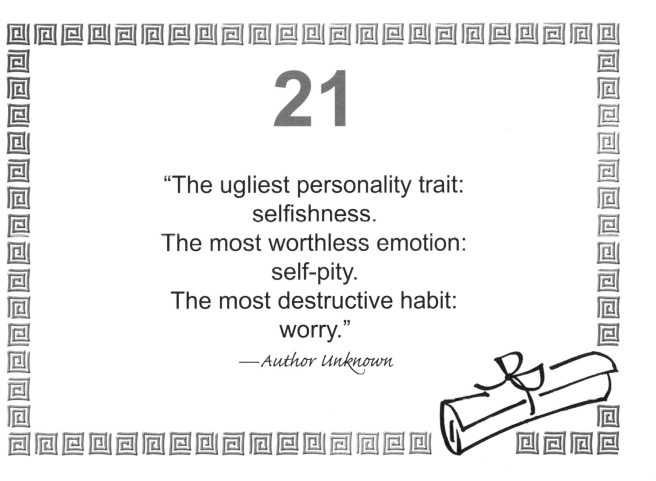

22

"I'm a great believer in luck,
and I find the harder I work,
the more I have of it."

— *Thomas Jefferson*

*"There are no shortcuts
to any place worth going."*
—*Beverly Sills*

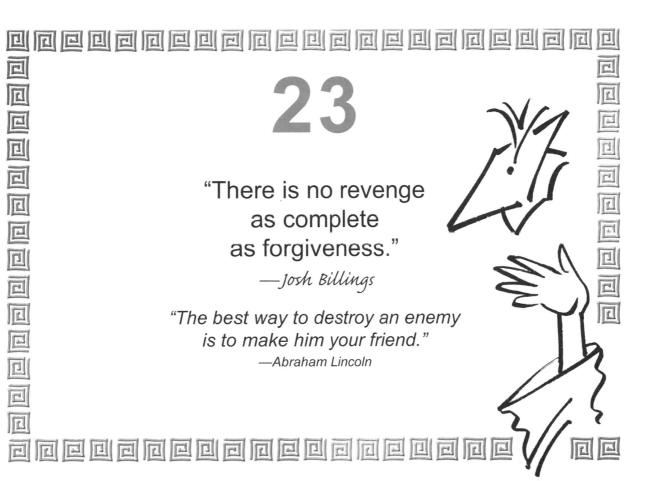

23

"There is no revenge
as complete
as forgiveness."
—*Josh Billings*

*"The best way to destroy an enemy
is to make him your friend."*
—*Abraham Lincoln*

24

"Remember that
great love and
great achievements
involve great risk."

—*H. Jackson Brown*

25

"Don't let little disputes injure a great friendship."

—*Author Unknown*

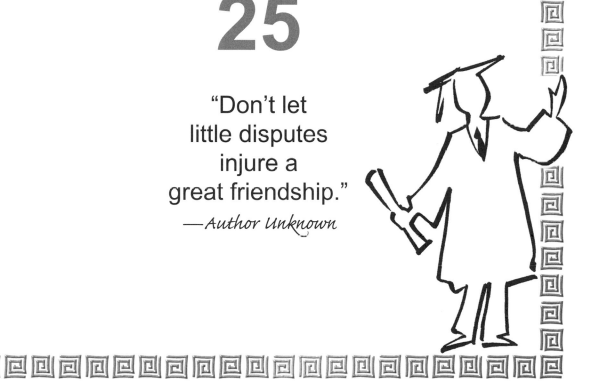

26

Stand up,
remove your hat
and place your hand
over your heart
during the playing
of the national anthem.

*Singing it loudly and proudly
is also appropriate.*

27

Give up your seat
to someone older than you,
or to someone
who is pregnant.

28

"The proof of integrity
is what you do
when no one is looking."

—*Denis Waitley*

29

Measure twice,
cut once.
Measure once,
cut twice.

30

"You can easily
judge the character of a person
by the way he deals with three things:
1. Rainy days
2. Lost luggage
3. Tangled Christmas tree lights."

—*Author Unknown*

*You can also tell a lot about a person
by how he treats the waiter or waitress.*

31

"You probably wouldn't worry so much about what other people think about you if you could only realize how seldom they do."

—Olin Miller

32

Never write
anything on paper
(or in an e-mail)
that you would
be ashamed
to have read aloud
in church or in court.

33

If you do something
you know you shouldn't do,
it will beat you home.

34

"It is better to
keep your mouth closed
and let people think you are a fool
than to open it
and remove all doubt."

—*Mark Twain*

35

God isn't interested
in your ability.
He's interested in
your availability.

36

Remember that nothing
takes the place of
or is appreciated as much
as a handwritten note,
especially a thank-you note.

37

You will not die
if your cell phone
is turned off.

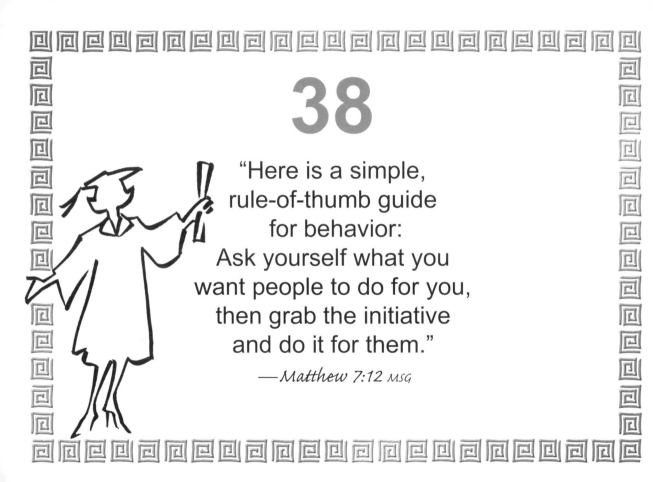

38

"Here is a simple,
rule-of-thumb guide
for behavior:
Ask yourself what you
want people to do for you,
then grab the initiative
and do it for them."

—*Matthew 7:12* MSG

39

"Don't take life
so seriously;
you will never
get out of it alive."

—*Elbert Hubbard*

40

Never burn a bridge;
you never know
when you might have to
cross back over it.

41

"Humility is
like underwear,
essential,
but indecent if it shows."

—*Helen Nielsen*

42

Don't get into a relationship
with someone you hope to change.
If they do change,
it most likely
won't be for the better.

43

"A good name
is more desirable
than great riches;
to be esteemed
is better than
silver or gold."

—Proverbs 22:1

Character does count.

44

"You can complain
because roses
have thorns,
or you can rejoice
because thorns
have roses."

— *Tom Wilson, from the comic strip "Ziggy"*

45

"How far you go in life
depends on your being tender
with the young, compassionate with the aged,
sympathetic with the striving,
and tolerant of the weak and strong—
because someday
you will have been all of these."

—*George Washington Carver*

Treat others kindly.

46

Don't be afraid to say:
I don't know
I made a mistake
I need help
I'm sorry
I love you

47

"Improve your performance by improving your attitude."

—*H. Jackson Brown*

"Life is 10 percent what happens and 90 percent how you react to it."
—*Charles R. Swindoll*

48

Never buy something
you don't need
just because it's on sale.

Extra money usually isn't extra very long.

49

Learn CPR and
the Heimlich maneuver.
You never know
when you may have
the opportunity
to save a life.

50

"You get
more flies
with honey
than vinegar."

—*Author Unknown*

51

Wash your hands.
It's the best defense
against illness.

*To further combat germs,
use your own pen,
especially in restaurants
and doctors' offices.*

52

When you are
overwhelmed with too much to do,
remember you don't have
to do it all at once.
Do the first thing.

God couldn't do it all in a day—what makes you think you can?

53

"Insanity is doing
the same thing
over and over and
expecting different results."

—*attributed to Albert Einstein*

54

"All things come to him who waits—
provided he knows what he is waiting for."

—*Woodrow Wilson*

*Be willing to wait for the new car,
the new house, the new cell phone
and always know that
those aren't the most important
things in life.*

55

Behave as if
God is always
watching you,
because
He is.

56

"Challenges are
inevitable.
Defeat is optional."

—*Roger Crawford*

57

"Most folks are
as happy as they
make up their minds to be."

—*Abraham Lincoln*

*No one can make you happy
but yourself.*

58

Don't let your possessions
possess you.

59

"If you think
your teacher is tough,
wait till you get a boss."

—*Charles J. Sykes*

60

Keep your promises.
If you can't,
then don't make them.

61

Don't let life discourage you;
everyone who
gets where he is
had to begin
where he was.

—*Ralph Waldo Emerson*

62

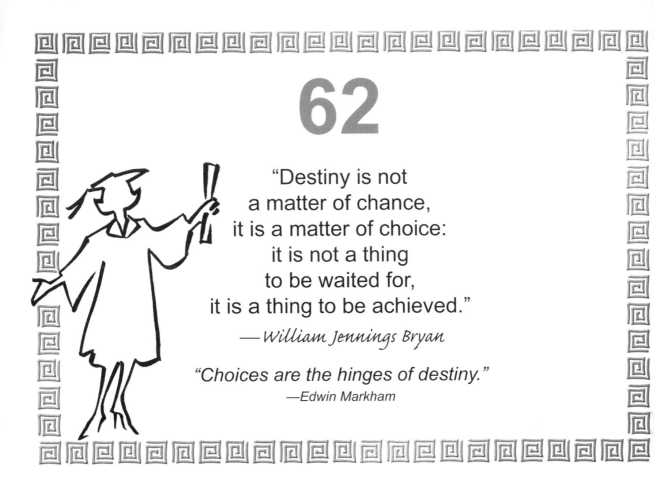

"Destiny is not
a matter of chance,
it is a matter of choice:
it is not a thing
to be waited for,
it is a thing to be achieved."

—*William Jennings Bryan*

"Choices are the hinges of destiny."
—*Edwin Markham*

63

"A pessimist is one
who makes difficulties
of his opportunities
and an optimist is
one who makes opportunities
of his difficulties."

—*Harry Truman*

*See the cup as half full
instead of half empty.*

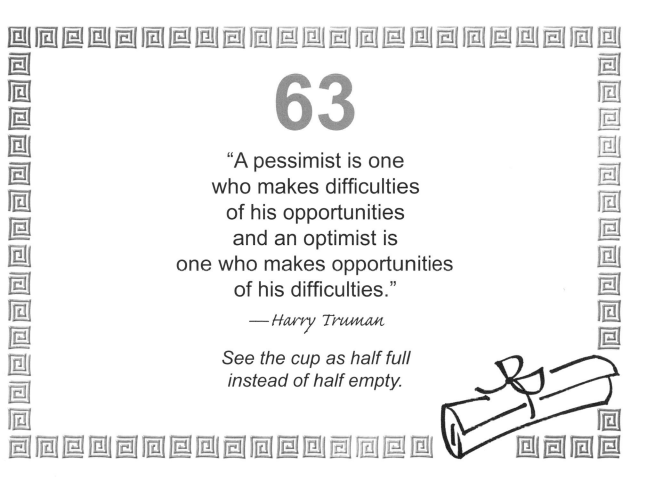

64

Tattoos are forever.
Try to visualize
what the tattoo will look like
when you are 75 years old.

65

"Happiness is like perfume;
you can't pour it
on someone else without getting
a few drops on yourself."

—*James Van Der Zee*

*Bring joy to someone else,
and you can't help but keep it for yourself.*

66

"The illiterate of the 21st century
will not be those who
cannot read and write,
but those who cannot learn,
unlearn and relearn."

—Alvin Toffler

67

Never let anyone
influence you
to do what
your heart
is telling you
not to do.

68

"You can't build
a reputation on what
you're going to do."

—*Henry Ford*

*"The smallest good deed
is better than the grandest good intention."*
—*Author Unknown*

69

"A merry heart doeth
good like a medicine."

—*Proverbs 17:22*

"Laughter is an instant vacation."
—*Milton Berle*

70

"Be careful of your actions because they become your habits and your habits become your character. Remember, your character determines your destiny."

—*Ancient Adage*

*"Bad habits are like a comfortable bed,
easy to get into, but hard to get out of."*
—*Author Unknown*

71

"Television ruins
more minds than drugs."

—*Author Unknown*

Don't be fooled.
Reality TV is not reality.

72

"A short pencil
is better than a long memory."

—*Author Unknown*

73

"The best sermons
are lived,
not preached."

—*Author Unknown*

74

"If you find
yourself in a hole,
stop digging."

—*Will Rogers*

75

"Let us endeavor
to live so that
when we come to die,
even the undertaker will be sorry."

—Mark Twain

76

"You can't get much done
in life if you only work
on the days when you feel good."

—*Basketball legend Jerry West*

*You can't choose how you feel,
but you can choose what to do about it.*

77

Vote.
It's a precious gift
paid for with the lives
of American soldiers.

Never underestimate the power of a single vote.

78

"For fast-acting relief,
try slowing down."

—Lily Tomlin

79

"Better to aim high
and miss the mark
than to
aim low
and make it."
—*Author Unknown*

*"Shoot for the moon. Even if you miss,
you'll land among the stars."*
—Les Brown

80

"You only get
one chance
to make a
bad first impression."

—*Author Unknown*

*So why not put in a little extra effort
and make a good one?*

81

Everyone is born
with a God-sized hole
in his heart.

82

Practice good manners.

Say "please" and "thank you."
Keep your elbows off the table, open the door for others,
stand when a woman enters the room.
And when eating at an elegant dinner party
and faced with more silverware than you've ever seen in your life,
watch the hostess.

83

Learn amazing grace.
Not the song,
though singing it will certainly
lift your spirits.
But learn to be graceful,
gracious, and grace-filled.

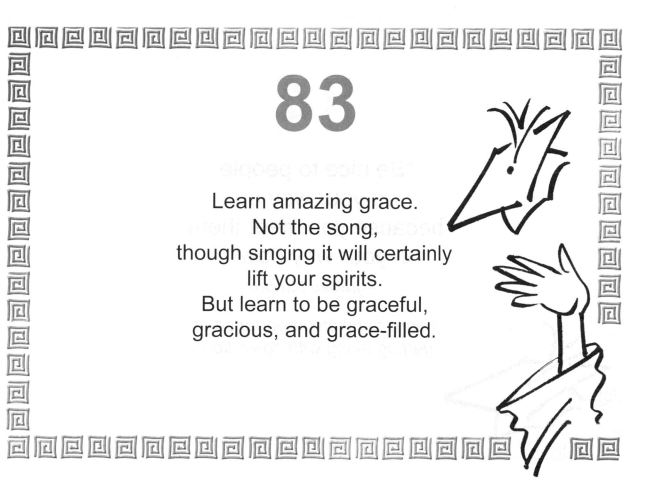

84

"Be nice to people
on your way up
because you meet them
on your way down."

—*Jimmy Durante*

*Learn early the importance of
getting along with coworkers.*

85

"The purpose
of life
is a life
of purpose."

— *Robert Byrne*

86

Learn to balance
your life
and your
checkbook.

Pay your credit card balances every month.
Debt is an ugly monster that robs you
of sleep, happiness, success,
and peace of mind.
A good credit rating is priceless.

87

Be glad that God
doesn't give you
everything you ask for.

88

"The easiest way
to grow as a person
is to surround yourself with people
who are smarter than you."

—*Author Unknown*

89

Appreciate
what you're given.

90

"All hard work
brings a profit,
but mere talk
leads only to poverty."

—*Proverbs 14:22–24*

Work smarter, not harder.

91

Don't play the
"blame game."

*If you do something wrong,
accept responsibility.*

92

"I've learned
that you shouldn't go
through life with a
catcher's mitt on both hands;
you need to be able
to throw something back."

—*Maya Angelou*

*"It's not what you gather,
but what you scatter that tells
what kind of life you have lived."*
—*Helen Walton*

93

"I am careful not to confuse excellence with perfection. Excellence, I can reach for; perfection is God's business."

— *Michael J. Fox*

94

"When you choose
the lesser of two evils,
always remember
that it is still an evil."

—*Max Lerner*

95

Be gentle
with the hearts
of others.

96

You will not go to jail
for tearing those
"Do Not Remove
Under Penalty of Law"
tags off the mattress.

*However, you will go to jail
for stealing, doing drugs,
or drinking and driving.*

97

"Blessed are those
who can laugh
at themselves,
for they shall
never cease
to be amused."

—*Author Unknown*

98

Do your work
so well
that it will
open doors
to new opportunities.

*Tasks done at a high standard
pave the way to bigger things.*

99

Make your parents
and your grandparents proud.

100

"In three words,
I can sum up everything
I've learned about life:
it goes on."

—*Robert Frost*

No matter what happens today, there's always a tomorrow.

101

(Write your own most important piece of advice for the graduate.)

_____

_____

_____

_____

_____

_____

_____

_____

—

Many special thanks to:

Dr. Stuart Gulley, the Builders Sunday School Class, Genesis Sunday School Class, Mary Will Thompson Sunday School Class, Tabard Book Club, Angela Groves, Perry Snyder, Steve Robinson, Marlene Wheeler, Darlene Stephens, Wendy Tyler, Sandy Abadie, Judy Adcock, Andrea Lovejoy, Sherri Brown, Mechelle Wheless, Graham Dukes, Susan Ferguson, Jan Mallory, Rev. Greg Porterfield, Sandy Cox, Nancy Durand, Laura Shedd, Susan Ducote, Bobby Carmichael, Keith Crusan, Pat Barns, Kelly Pridgen, Denise Galster, Marty Young, Jan Oliver, Bill Evans, Joyce Self, Helen Middlebrooks, Vanessa Railey, Shirra Rogers, Fran Nichols, Georgia Thompson, Catherine Holmes, Pam Culberson, Kelly Ricker, Todd Willis, Nadine Abbott, Barbara Claborn, Laura Jennings, and many others who contributed words of wisdom and whose names I may have failed to mention.